THE THOUGHTS OF MY PUG

Weekly Planner 2020

2020

January
S	M	T	W	T	F	S
			1	2	3	4
5	6	7	8	9	10	11
12	13	14	15	16	17	18
19	20	21	22	23	24	25
26	27	28	29	30	31	

February
S	M	T	W	T	F	S
						1
2	3	4	5	6	7	8
9	10	11	12	13	14	15
16	17	18	19	20	21	22
23	24	25	26	27	28	29

March
S	M	T	W	T	F	S
1	2	3	4	5	6	7
8	9	10	11	12	13	14
15	16	17	18	19	20	21
22	23	24	25	26	27	28
29	30	31				

April
S	M	T	W	T	F	S
			1	2	3	4
5	6	7	8	9	10	11
12	13	14	15	16	17	18
19	20	21	22	23	24	25
26	27	28	29	30		

May
S	M	T	W	T	F	S
					1	2
3	4	5	6	7	8	9
10	11	12	13	14	15	16
17	18	19	20	21	22	23
24	25	26	27	28	29	30
31						

June
S	M	T	W	T	F	S
	1	2	3	4	5	6
7	8	9	10	11	12	13
14	15	16	17	18	19	20
21	22	23	24	25	26	27
28	29	30				

July
S	M	T	W	T	F	S
			1	2	3	4
5	6	7	8	9	10	11
12	13	14	15	16	17	18
19	20	21	22	23	24	25
26	27	28	29	30	31	

August
S	M	T	W	T	F	S
						1
2	3	4	5	6	7	8
9	10	11	12	13	14	15
16	17	18	19	20	21	22
23	24	25	26	27	28	29
30	31					

September
S	M	T	W	T	F	S
		1	2	3	4	5
6	7	8	9	10	11	12
13	14	15	16	17	18	19
20	21	22	23	24	25	26
27	28	29	30			

October
S	M	T	W	T	F	S
				1	2	3
4	5	6	7	8	9	10
11	12	13	14	15	16	17
18	19	20	21	22	23	24
25	26	27	28	29	30	31

November
S	M	T	W	T	F	S
1	2	3	4	5	6	7
8	9	10	11	12	13	14
15	16	17	18	19	20	21
22	23	24	25	26	27	28
29	30					

December
S	M	T	W	T	F	S
		1	2	3	4	5
6	7	8	9	10	11	12
13	14	15	16	17	18	19
20	21	22	23	24	25	26
27	28	29	30	31		

2021

January
S	M	T	W	T	F	S
					1	2
3	4	5	6	7	8	9
10	11	12	13	14	15	16
17	18	19	20	21	22	23
24	25	26	27	28	29	30
31						

February
S	M	T	W	T	F	S
	1	2	3	4	5	6
7	8	9	10	11	12	13
14	15	16	17	18	19	20
21	22	23	24	25	26	27
28						

March
S	M	T	W	T	F	S
	1	2	3	4	5	6
7	8	9	10	11	12	13
14	15	16	17	18	19	20
21	22	23	24	25	26	27
28	29	30	31			

April
S	M	T	W	T	F	S
				1	2	3
4	5	6	7	8	9	10
11	12	13	14	15	16	17
18	19	20	21	22	23	24
25	26	27	28	29	30	

May
S	M	T	W	T	F	S
						1
2	3	4	5	6	7	8
9	10	11	12	13	14	15
16	17	18	19	20	21	22
23	24	25	26	27	28	29
30	31					

June
S	M	T	W	T	F	S
		1	2	3	4	5
6	7	8	9	10	11	12
13	14	15	16	17	18	19
20	21	22	23	24	25	26
27	28	29	30			

July
S	M	T	W	T	F	S
				1	2	3
4	5	6	7	8	9	10
11	12	13	14	15	16	17
18	19	20	21	22	23	24
25	26	27	28	29	30	31

August
S	M	T	W	T	F	S
1	2	3	4	5	6	7
8	9	10	11	12	13	14
15	16	17	18	19	20	21
22	23	24	25	26	27	28
29	30	31				

September
S	M	T	W	T	F	S
			1	2	3	4
5	6	7	8	9	10	11
12	13	14	15	16	17	18
19	20	21	22	23	24	25
26	27	28	29	30		

October
S	M	T	W	T	F	S
					1	2
3	4	5	6	7	8	9
10	11	12	13	14	15	16
17	18	19	20	21	22	23
24	25	26	27	28	29	30
31						

November
S	M	T	W	T	F	S
	1	2	3	4	5	6
7	8	9	10	11	12	13
14	15	16	17	18	19	20
21	22	23	24	25	26	27
28	29	30				

December
S	M	T	W	T	F	S
			1	2	3	4
5	6	7	8	9	10	11
12	13	14	15	16	17	18
19	20	21	22	23	24	25
26	27	28	29	30	31	

DOGGY LANGUAGE

There's an entire language devoted to dogs; this language is known as Doggo Lingo. It's how your dog speaks and thinks. It's a fun, positive celebration of dogs.

Doggo	Doggos come in a variety of sizes ranked by the size of their bork (bark). They range from the tiny yapper to a diminutive pupper, an average-sized doggo, and the biggest woofers and boofers.
Longboi	A long-bodied dog such as a greyhound.
Floofer/Fluffer	A very fluffy dog such as a Samoyed or Pomeranian.
Thicc boi	A chubby dog – more to love.
Smol boi	A little yapper.
Woofer	A big dog.
Loaf	A dog, slightly overweight, which resembles a loaf of bread.
Pupper	A puppy.
Heckin' bamboozled	Sometimes you bamboozle the dog, sometimes the dog bamboozles you. Heck.
Do me a frighten	When a doggo is worried, scared or confused, potentially in the presence of borks or woofers.
Doin' me a	Having an action performed on oneself.
Bamboozle	A deceiving trick.
Awoo!	Howling.
Hooman	A human being.

DOGGY LANGUAGE

Blep/Blop	When your pupper is tired and his tongue hangs out just a little bit.
Mlem	Doing a lick. Not to be confused with a gentle blop.
Bork	Barking his little head off.
Boof	Not quite a bork, not quite a sneeze; it's the small huffy sound of a dog who's getting ready to bork..
Maximum borkdrive	This is otherwise known as the zoomies, when your doggo is going so fast they're just a blur.
Chimken	Chicken.
Fren	Friend
Henlo	Hello
Snoot	The nose always knows, and the snoot was made for booping.
Boop!	Touching your pet on the nose. Frequently accompanied by saying 'boop!'

Me and the hooman and the new fren went for a walk. And we saw other woofers and I jumped into a mud puddle. Awoo!

About My Dog

Dog's Name: ....

Date of Birth: ....

Breed: ....

Colour: ....

Gender: ....

Adoption Date: ....

Weight: ....

Breeder: ....

Microchip No: ....

Registration No: ....

Rabies: ....

Neutered/Speyed: ....

JANUARY 2020

Sun	Mon	Tue	Wed	Thu	Fri	Sat
29	30	31	1	2	3	4
5	6	7	8	9	10	11
12	13	14	15	16	17	18
19	20	21	22	23	24	25
26	27	28	29	30	31	1

Notes:

Week Beginning: December 30, 2020

	MONDAY
TUESDAY	
WEDNESDAY	
THURSDAY	
FRIDAY	
SATURDAY	
SUNDAY	

TOP PRIORITIES

VARIOUS TO DO

PEOPLE TO CONNECT WITH

PLACES TO VISIT

THINGS FOR NEXT WEEK

M December 30

Remember!

T December 31

Remember!

W January 1

Remember!

Th January 2

Remember!

F January 3

Remember!

S January 4

January 5 **S**

Week Beginning: January 6, 2020

MONDAY

TUESDAY

WEDNESDAY

THURSDAY

FRIDAY

SATURDAY

SUNDAY

TOP PRIORITIES

VARIOUS TO DO

PEOPLE TO CONNECT WITH

PLACES TO VISIT

THINGS FOR NEXT WEEK

M January 6

Remember!

T January 7

Remember!

W January 8

Remember!

Th January 9

Remember!

F January 10

Remember!

S January 11

January 12 S

Week Beginning: January 13, 2020

MONDAY	
TUESDAY	
WEDNESDAY	
THURSDAY	
FRIDAY	
SATURDAY	
SUNDAY	

TOP PRIORITIES

VARIOUS TO DO

PEOPLE TO CONNECT WITH

PLACES TO VISIT

THINGS FOR NEXT WEEK

M January 13

T January 14

Remember!

Remember!

W January 15

Th January 16

Remember!

Remember!

F January 17

S January 18

January 19 **S**

Remember!

Week Beginning: January 20, 2020

MONDAY

TUESDAY

WEDNESDAY

THURSDAY

FRIDAY

SATURDAY

SUNDAY

TOP PRIORITIES

VARIOUS TO DO

PEOPLE TO CONNECT WITH

PLACES TO VISIT

THINGS FOR NEXT WEEK

M January 20

Remember!

T January 21

Remember!

W January 22

Remember!

Th January 23

Remember!

F January 24

Remember!

S January 25

January 26 **S**

Week Beginning: January 27, 2020

MONDAY

TUESDAY

WEDNESDAY

THURSDAY

FRIDAY

SATURDAY

SUNDAY

---------- TOP PRIORITIES ----------

VARIOUS TO DO

PEOPLE TO CONNECT WITH

PLACES TO VISIT

THINGS FOR NEXT WEEK

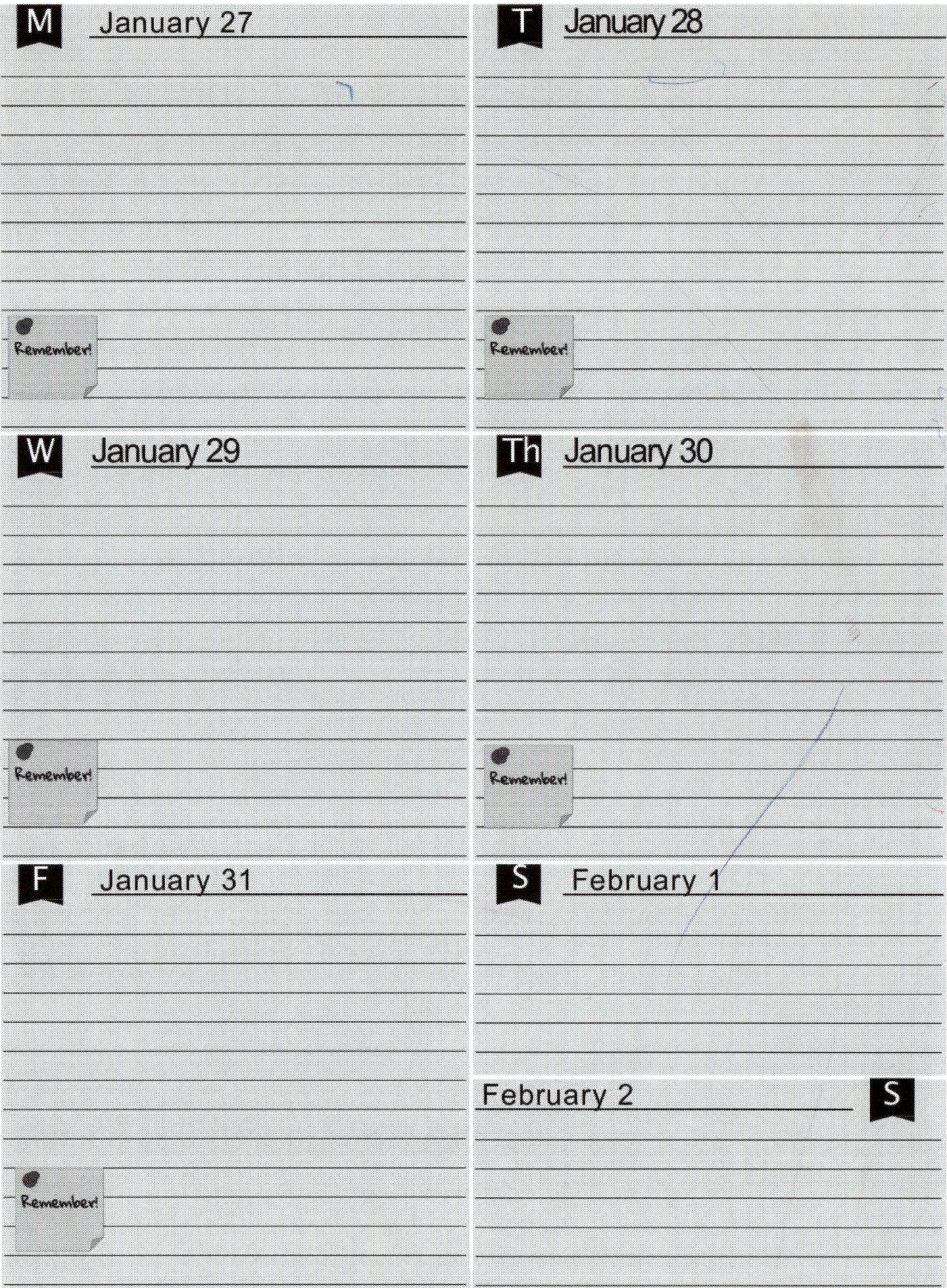

Notes…

Easy Doggie Donuts

Ingredients:
1 cup flour
1 cup oats
1/3 cup coconut oil
1/2 cup peanut Butter
2 Eggs

For the topping:
Greek Yogurt
Bacon Bits

Directions:

Preheat your oven to 375 degrees. Spray a donut pan with cooking spray and set aside.

In a large bowl, combine all ingredients (except yogurt and bacon bits). You can mix with a spoon or use your hands (super fun for kids!). Mix until a dough forms. Use your hands to press the dough into the donut pan. Fill each donut cavity and press firmly to ensure everything sticks together (it won't rise, so you should make sure each space is tightly packed).

Bake in your preheated oven at 375 degrees for approximately 14 mins or until cooked completely.

Allow to cool, then carefully remove the donuts from the pan. Now you're ready to decorate them!

Set out a small bowl of plan Greek yogurt and another of bacon bits. Dip each donut carefully in the yogurt, then sprinkle with bacon bits.

Place your finished donuts in the freezer for a few moments to harden the yogurt. My dogs like to eat them straight from the freezer, but you can also store in the refrigerator. Just keep in mind that the yogurt may get a little sticky.

January Photo

Noise has woken me. Possible causes...
...world ending
...no other possibilities
...definite catastrophe
...wake the hooman!

NOW!

FEBRUARY

Dogs' lives are too short. It's their only fault

FEBRUARY 2020

Sun	Mon	Tue	Wed	Thu	Fri	Sat
26	27	28	29	30	31	1
2	3	4	5	6	7	8
9	10	11	12	13	14	15
16	17	18	19	20	21	22
23	24	25	26	27	28	29

Notes:

Week Beginning: February 3, 2020

MONDAY

TUESDAY

WEDNESDAY

THURSDAY

FRIDAY

SATURDAY

SUNDAY

TOP PRIORITIES

VARIOUS TO DO

PEOPLE TO CONNECT WITH

PLACES TO VISIT

THINGS FOR NEXT WEEK

M February 3

Remember!

T February 4

Remember!

W February 5

Remember!

Th February 6

Remember!

F February 7

Remember!

S February 8

February 9 **S**

Week Beginning: February 10, 2020

	MONDAY
	TUESDAY
	WEDNESDAY
	THURSDAY
	FRIDAY
	SATURDAY
	SUNDAY

TOP PRIORITIES

VARIOUS TO DO

PEOPLE TO CONNECT WITH

PLACES TO VISIT

THINGS FOR NEXT WEEK

M February 10

T February 11

Remember!

Remember!

W February 12

Th February 13

Remember!

Remember!

F February 14

S February 15

February 16 **S**

Remember!

Week Beginning: February 17, 2020

MONDAY
TUESDAY
WEDNESDAY
THURSDAY
FRIDAY
SATURDAY
SUNDAY

TOP PRIORITIES

VARIOUS TO DO

PEOPLE TO CONNECT WITH

PLACES TO VISIT

THINGS FOR NEXT WEEK

| **M** | February 17 |
| **T** | February 18 |

Remember!

| **W** | February 19 |
| **Th** | February 20 |

Remember!

| **F** | February 21 |
| **S** | February 22 |

February 23 | **S**

Remember!

Week Beginning: February 24, 2020

	MONDAY
	TUESDAY
	WEDNESDAY
	THURSDAY
	FRIDAY
	SATURDAY
	SUNDAY

TOP PRIORITIES

VARIOUS TO DO

PEOPLE TO CONNECT WITH

PLACES TO VISIT

THINGS FOR NEXT WEEK

M February 24

Remember!

T February 25

Remember!

W February 26

Remember!

Th February 27

Remember!

F February 28

Remember!

S February 29

March 1 **S**

Notes…

Bacon & Peanut Butter Glaze

Ingredients:

Dog biscuits:
- 1 cup pumpkin
- 1/2 cup peanut butter
- 2 eggs
- 1/4 cup oil
- 2 1/2 cups whole wheat flour
- 1 teaspoon baking soda

Glaze:
- 2 tablespoons bacon grease, coconut oil, chicken fat, or any other fat that will solidify at room temperature, melted
- 1/4 cup smooth peanut butter

Instructions:

Preheat oven to 350 degrees.

Combine pumpkin, peanut butter, eggs, and oil in a bowl. Add in baking soda and whole wheat flour. Stir until a stiff dough forms. Knead dough or mix just until flour is incorporated.

Roll out dough with a rolling pin and use a cookie cutter to cut out dog bone shapes, or just bake into little circles like cookies. Bake for 15 minutes.

Whisk the bacon grease and peanut butter until very smooth. Drizzle over the treats and cool till glaze hardens (it does best in the fridge or freezer).

Please check with your vet or use an alternative type of oil if you are concerned about bacon grease.

February Photo

A new week is upon us....
Or so the hooman tells me.
Hooman time constructs do me a bamboozle. I prefer to break it down into snoozes, non snoozes and.......

MAXIMUM BORKDRIVE

MARCH 2020

Sun	Mon	Tue	Wed	Thu	Fri	Sat
1	2	3	4	5	6	7
8	9	10	11	12	13	14
15	16	17	18	19	20	21
22	23	24	25	26	27	28
29	30	31	1	2	3	4

Notes:

Week Beginning March 2, 2020

MONDAY	
TUESDAY	
WEDNESDAY	
THURSDAY	
FRIDAY	
SATURDAY	
SUNDAY	

TOP PRIORITIES

VARIOUS TO DO

PEOPLE TO CONNECT WITH

PLACES TO VISIT

THINGS FOR NEXT WEEK

M March 2

T March 3

W March 4

Th March 5

F March 6

S March 7

March 8 **S**

Week Beginning March 9, 2020

MONDAY	
TUESDAY	
WEDNESDAY	
THURSDAY	
FRIDAY	
SATURDAY	
SUNDAY	

TOP PRIORITIES

VARIOUS TO DO

PEOPLE TO CONNECT WITH

PLACES TO VISIT

THINGS FOR NEXT WEEK

M March 9

Remember!

T March 10

Remember!

W March 11

Remember!

Th March 12

Remember!

F March 13

Remember!

S March 14

March 15 **S**

Week Beginning March 16, 2020

MONDAY	
TUESDAY	
WEDNESDAY	
THURSDAY	
FRIDAY	
SATURDAY	
SUNDAY	

TOP PRIORITIES

VARIOUS TO DO

PEOPLE TO CONNECT WITH

PLACES TO VISIT

THINGS FOR NEXT WEEK

M March 16

T March 17

W March 18

Th March 19

F March 20

S March 21

March 22 **S**

Week Beginning March 23, 2020

MONDAY

TUESDAY

WEDNESDAY

THURSDAY

FRIDAY

SATURDAY

SUNDAY

TOP PRIORITIES

VARIOUS TO DO

PEOPLE TO CONNECT WITH

PLACES TO VISIT

THINGS FOR NEXT WEEK

M March 23

T March 24

Remember!

Remember!

W March 25

Th March 26

Remember!

Remember!

F March 27

S March 28

March 29 **S**

Remember!

Week Beginning March 30, 2020

MONDAY	
TUESDAY	
WEDNESDAY	
THURSDAY	
FRIDAY	
SATURDAY	
SUNDAY	

TOP PRIORITIES

VARIOUS TO DO

PEOPLE TO CONNECT WITH

PLACES TO VISIT

THINGS FOR NEXT WEEK

M March 30

T March 31

Remember!

Remember!

W April 1

Th April 2

Remember!

Remember!

F April 3

S April 4

April 5 **S**

Remember!

Notes…

Spinach, Carrot & Zucchini Treats

Ingredients:
- 1 cup pumpkin puree
- 1/4 cup peanut butter
- 2 large eggs
- 1/2 cup old fashioned oats
- 3 cups whole wheat flour, or more, as needed
- 1 carrot, peeled and shredded
- 1 zucchini, shredded
- 1 cup baby spinach, chopped

Instructions:

Preheat oven to 350 degrees F. Line a baking sheet with parchment paper or a silicone baking mat; set aside.

In the bowl of an electric mixer fitted with the paddle attachment, beat pumpkin puree, peanut butter and eggs on medium-high until well combined, about 1-2 minutes.

Gradually add old fashioned oats and 2 1/2 cups flour at low speed, beating just until incorporated. Add an additional 1/4 cup flour at a time just until the dough is no longer sticky. Add carrot, zucchini and spinach, beating just until incorporated.

Working on a lightly floured surface, knead the dough 3-4 times until it comes together. Using a rolling pin, roll the dough to 1/4-inch thickness. Using cookie cutters, cut out desired shapes and place onto the prepared baking sheet.

Place into oven and bake until the edges are golden brown, about 20-25 minutes. Let cool completely.

March Photo

Sometimes, I grrbork at the sky... in case anybody is listening.
You ever wake up in the middle of the night and think...why?

I NEED CHIMKIN!

APRIL 2020

Sun	Mon	Tue	Wed	Thu	Fri	Sat
29	30	31	1	2	3	4
5	6	7	8	9	10	11
12	13	14	15	16	17	18
19	20	21	22	23	24	25
26	27	28	29	30	1	2

Notes:

Week Beginning April 6, 2020

MONDAY	
TUESDAY	
WEDNESDAY	
THURSDAY	
FRIDAY	
SATURDAY	
SUNDAY	

TOP PRIORITIES

VARIOUS TO DO

PEOPLE TO CONNECT WITH

PLACES TO VISIT

THINGS FOR NEXT WEEK

M April 6

Remember!

T April 7

Remember!

W April 8

Remember!

Th April 9

Remember!

F April 10

Remember!

S April 11

April 12 **S**

Week Beginning April 13, 2020

	MONDAY
	TUESDAY
	WEDNESDAY
	THURSDAY
	FRIDAY
	SATURDAY
	SUNDAY

TOP PRIORITIES

VARIOUS TO DO

PEOPLE TO CONNECT WITH

PLACES TO VISIT

THINGS FOR NEXT WEEK

M April 13

Remember!

T April 14

Remember!

W April 15

Remember!

Th April 16

Remember!

F April 17

Remember!

S April 18

April 19 **S**

Week Beginning April 20, 2020

MONDAY	
TUESDAY	
WEDNESDAY	
THURSDAY	
FRIDAY	
SATURDAY	
SUNDAY	

TOP PRIORITIES

VARIOUS TO DO

PEOPLE TO CONNECT WITH

PLACES TO VISIT

THINGS FOR NEXT WEEK

| **M** April 20 | **T** April 21 |

Remember!

| **W** April 22 | **Th** April 23 |

Remember!

| **F** April 24 | **S** April 25 |

April 26 **S**

Remember!

Week Beginning April 27, 2020

MONDAY

TUESDAY

WEDNESDAY

THURSDAY

FRIDAY

SATURDAY

SUNDAY

---------- TOP PRIORITIES ----------

VARIOUS TO DO

PEOPLE TO CONNECT WITH

PLACES TO VISIT

THINGS FOR NEXT WEEK

M April 27

Remember!

T April 28

Remember!

W April 29

Remember!

Th April 30

Remember!

F May 1

Remember!

S May 2

May 3 **S**

MY ZOOMIES ARE IMPROVING... I KNOW THIS BECAUSE THE PHOTOS ARE GETTING MORE BLURRY!

Notes…

Bacon Cheddar Treats

Ingredients:
- 1 ½ cups rolled oats
- ½ cup shredded cheddar cheese
- 4 strips bacon, cooked and crumbled
- 2 eggs

Instructions:

Preheat oven to 350 degrees Fahrenheit.
Add oats, cheese, and bacon to the bowl of a food processor and process until ingredients reach a crumb-like consistency.
Add two eggs to food processor and process until mixture resembles a sticky dough.
Sprinkle flour or finely ground oats onto a wood cutting board and roll out dough to about ¼-inch thick. Using a cookie cutter, cut out dough into desired shape.
Transfer dog treats to a parchment-lined baking sheet and cook for 20 minutes.
Cool treats completely and store in an airtight glass or plastic container.

April Photo

Guys, I just had a morning walk. Some big doggo borked at me and I almost caught Bruce, the lizard.

LIFE IS GOOD!

MAY 2020

Sun	Mon	Tue	Wed	Thu	Fri	Sat
26	27	28	29	30	1	2
3	4	5	6	7	8	9
10	11	12	13	14	15	16
17	18	19	20	21	22	23
24	25	26	27	28	29	30
31	1	2	3	4	5	6

Notes:

Week Beginning May 4, 2020

MONDAY

TUESDAY

WEDNESDAY

THURSDAY

FRIDAY

SATURDAY

SUNDAY

TOP PRIORITIES

VARIOUS TO DO

PEOPLE TO CONNECT WITH

PLACES TO VISIT

THINGS FOR NEXT WEEK

M May 4

T May 5

Remember!

Remember!

W May 6

Th May 7

Remember!

Remember!

F May 8

S May 9

May 10 **S**

Remember!

Week Beginning May 11, 2020

MONDAY	
TUESDAY	
WEDNESDAY	
THURSDAY	
FRIDAY	
SATURDAY	
SUNDAY	

TOP PRIORITIES

VARIOUS TO DO

PEOPLE TO CONNECT WITH

PLACES TO VISIT

THINGS FOR NEXT WEEK

M May 11

T May 12

Remember!

Remember!

W May 13

Th May 14

Remember!

Remember!

F May 15

S May 16

May 17 **S**

Remember!

Week Beginning May 18, 2020

MONDAY	
TUESDAY	
WEDNESDAY	
THURSDAY	
FRIDAY	
SATURDAY	
SUNDAY	

TOP PRIORITIES

VARIOUS TO DO

PEOPLE TO CONNECT WITH

PLACES TO VISIT

THINGS FOR NEXT WEEK

M May 18

T May 19

Remember!

Remember!

W May 20

Th May 21

Remember!

Remember!

F May 22

S May 23

May 24 **S**

Remember!

Week Beginning May 25, 2020

MONDAY	
TUESDAY	
WEDNESDAY	
THURSDAY	
FRIDAY	
SATURDAY	
SUNDAY	

TOP PRIORITIES

VARIOUS TO DO

PEOPLE TO CONNECT WITH

PLACES TO VISIT

THINGS FOR NEXT WEEK

M May 25

Remember!

T May 26

Remember!

W May 27

Remember!

Th May 28

Remember!

F May 29

Remember!

S May 30

May 31 **S**

THE GARAGE HAS OPENED...
THE HOOMAN IS HOME!!!
MAXIMUM BORKDRIVE...
I AM SO EXCITED.

Notes…

Chicken & Wild Rice Biscuits

Ingredients:

- Start off by boiling a piece of boneless chicken breast and making wild rice; then allowed them to cool. You can do this a day ahead and keep refrigerated until ready to use.
- Puree the chicken and rice with some chicken stock in a mini food processor or blender
- Add flour, salt, egg and pureed chicken and rice to a bowl and mix well; then roll out the dough on a lightly floured board until 1/2-inch thick.
- You can use any cookie cutter or glass to cut out the biscuits.
- Once you cut out the shapes, bake for about 30 minutes; then allow to harden.

Instructions:

Preheat oven to 350 degrees F.

Combine chicken, rice and chicken stock in a mini food processor or blender and pulse until a paste forms.

Add the flour, salt, egg and chicken paste into a bowl and mix well.

Sprinkle a little flour on a flat surface and knead dough until it's no longer sticky; then roll it out with a rolling pin about 1/2-inch thick.

Cut out shapes and place them on a parchment paper lined baking sheet.

Mine yielded 32 biscuits using a 3.5" cookie cutter.

Bake for 25-30 minutes until light brown. Remove from oven and allow to cool completely before serving.

Chicken & Wild Rice Biscuits

Keep these biscuits in an airtight container for up to one week. These biscuits can be stored in an airtight container in the freezer for up to 6 months. Allow to defrost completely (10-20 minutes) before serving.

May Photo

Human gave me an extra long hug and direct eye contact. These are heckin' signals. We're on the same page.

I FEEL CHIMKIN COMING!

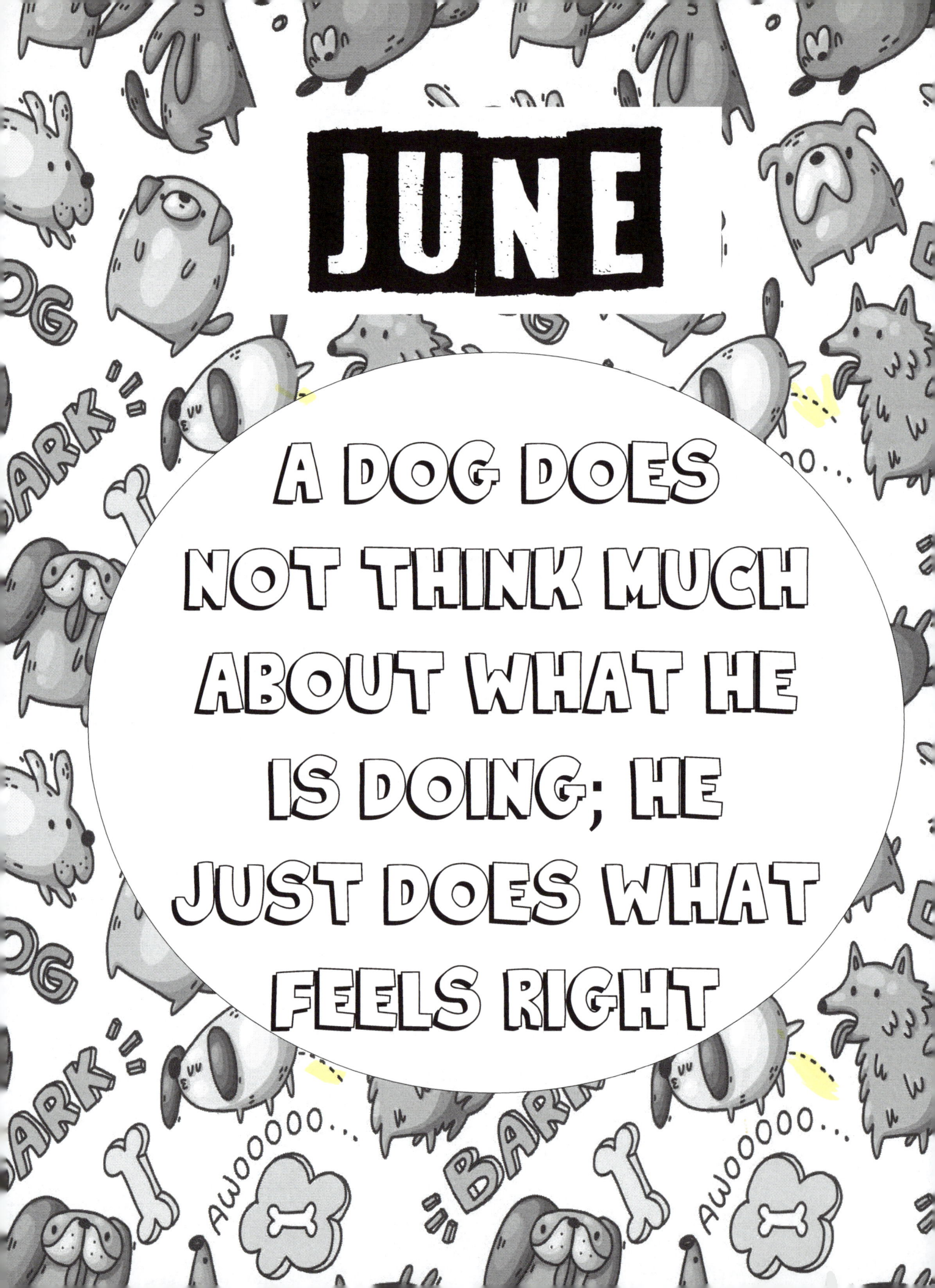

JUNE 2020

Sun	Mon	Tue	Wed	Thu	Fri	Sat
31	1	2	3	4	5	6
7	8	9	10	11	12	13
14	15	16	17	18	19	20
21	22	23	24	25	26	27
28	29	30	1	2	3	4

Notes:

Cranberry Cookies

- **Ingredients:**
- 2 eggs
- 1.5 cups almond flour
- 1 Tablespoon coconut oil
- 3-4 Tablespoons coconut flour
- 1/2 cup dried cranberries

Instructions:

Preheat oven to 325 degrees.

Beat the eggs and set aside.

Combine almond flour, coconut oil, and dried cranberries in a bowl.

Add in the eggs and knead the ingredients with your hands. Dough will be wet and sticky.

Add in the coconut flour one tablespoon at a time to achieve a consistency that is easy to roll out and not overly sticky. This should take approximately 3-4 TBSP.

Roll out the dough and cut out the treats using heart shaped cookie cutters. Place the treats on a cookie sheet lined with parchment paper.

Bake for 15-18 minutes or until crisp.

Week Beginning June 1, 2020

MONDAY
TUESDAY
WEDNESDAY
THURSDAY
FRIDAY
SATURDAY
SUNDAY

TOP PRIORITIES

VARIOUS TO DO

PEOPLE TO CONNECT WITH

PLACES TO VISIT

THINGS FOR NEXT WEEK

M June 1

Remember!

T June 2

Remember!

W June 3

Remember!

Th June 4

Remember!

F June 5

Remember!

S June 6

June 7 **S**

Week Beginning June 8, 2020

MONDAY	
TUESDAY	
WEDNESDAY	
THURSDAY	
FRIDAY	
SATURDAY	
SUNDAY	

TOP PRIORITIES

VARIOUS TO DO

PEOPLE TO CONNECT WITH

PLACES TO VISIT

THINGS FOR NEXT WEEK

M June 8

T June 9

Remember!

Remember!

W June 10

Th June 11

Remember!

Remember!

F June 12

S June 13

June 14 **S**

Remember!

Week Beginning June 15, 2020

MONDAY	
TUESDAY	
WEDNESDAY	
THURSDAY	
FRIDAY	
SATURDAY	
SUNDAY	

TOP PRIORITIES

VARIOUS TO DO

PEOPLE TO CONNECT WITH

PLACES TO VISIT

THINGS FOR NEXT WEEK

M June 15

Remember!

T June 16

Remember!

W June 17

Remember!

Th June 18

Remember!

F June 19

Remember!

S June 20

June 21 **S**

Week Beginning June 22, 2020

MONDAY	
TUESDAY	
WEDNESDAY	
THURSDAY	
FRIDAY	
SATURDAY	
SUNDAY	

TOP PRIORITIES

VARIOUS TO DO

PEOPLE TO CONNECT WITH

PLACES TO VISIT

THINGS FOR NEXT WEEK

M June 22	**T** June 23
Remember!	Remember!

W June 24	**Th** June 25
Remember!	Remember!

F June 26	**S** June 27
	June 28 **S**
Remember!	

Week Beginning June 29, 2020

MONDAY	
TUESDAY	
WEDNESDAY	
THURSDAY	
FRIDAY	
SATURDAY	
SUNDAY	

TOP PRIORITIES

VARIOUS TO DO

PEOPLE TO CONNECT WITH

PLACES TO VISIT

THINGS FOR NEXT WEEK

M June 29

Remember!

T June 30

Remember!

W July 1

Remember!

Th July 2

Remember!

F July 3

Remember!

S July 4

July 5 **S**

When my hooman is not around to distract me, that's when I think my deepest thoughts...

Notes…

June Photo

I have been programming my hooman. Every time they give me food, I bork. Eventually, every time I bork, they will give me food.

I WANT CHEESE!

JULY 2020

Sun	Mon	Tue	Wed	Thu	Fri	Sat
28	29	30	1	2	3	4
5	6	7	8	9	10	11
12	13	14	15	16	17	18
19	20	21	22	23	24	25
26	27	28	29	30	31	1

Notes:

Week Beginning July 6, 2020

MONDAY
TUESDAY
WEDNESDAY
THURSDAY
FRIDAY
SATURDAY
SUNDAY

TOP PRIORITIES

VARIOUS TO DO

PEOPLE TO CONNECT WITH

PLACES TO VISIT

THINGS FOR NEXT WEEK

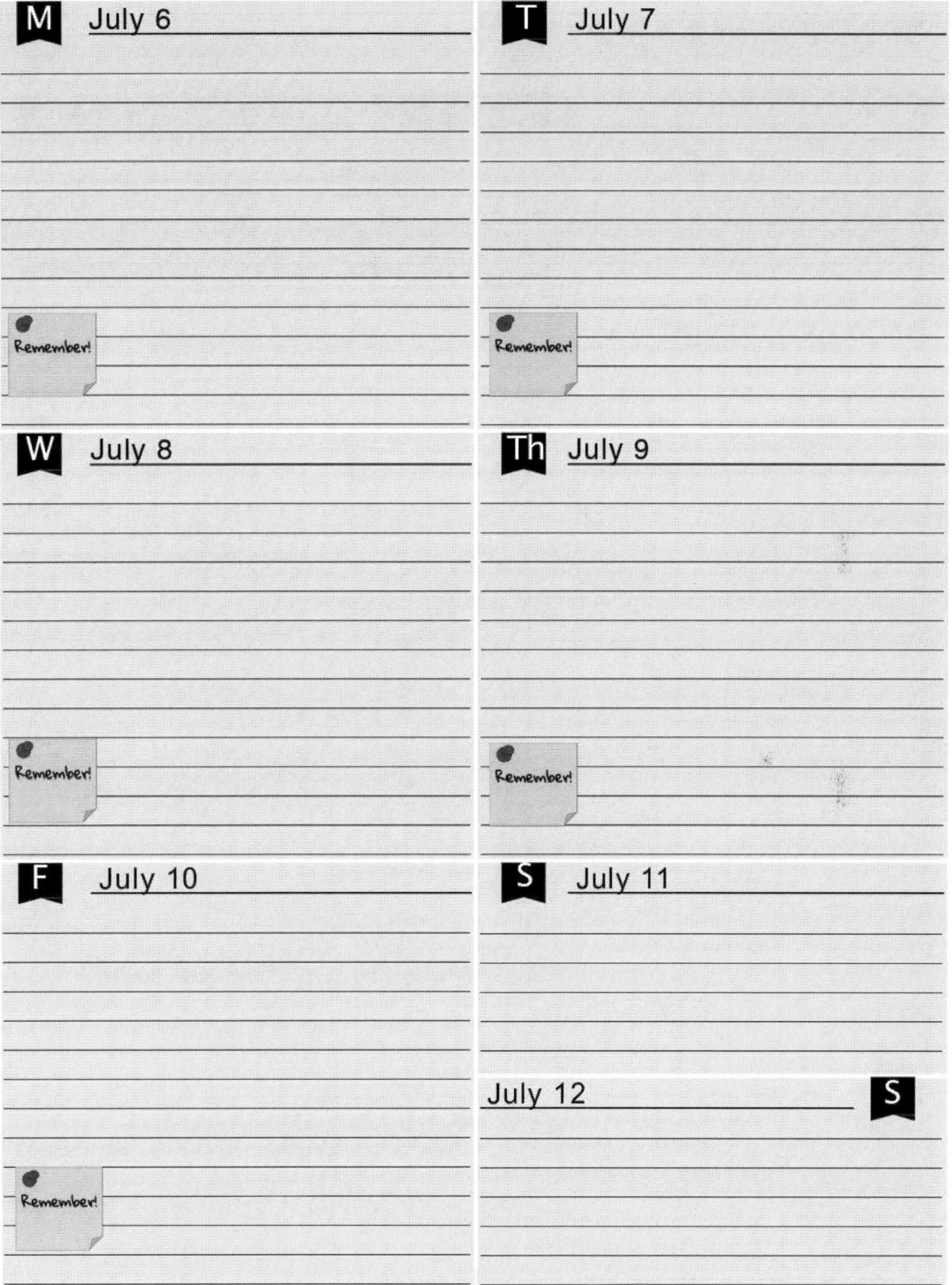

Week Beginning July 13, 2020

MONDAY	
TUESDAY	
WEDNESDAY	
THURSDAY	
FRIDAY	
SATURDAY	
SUNDAY	

TOP PRIORITIES

VARIOUS TO DO

PEOPLE TO CONNECT WITH

PLACES TO VISIT

THINGS FOR NEXT WEEK

Week Beginning July 20, 2020

MONDAY	
TUESDAY	
WEDNESDAY	
THURSDAY	
FRIDAY	
SATURDAY	
SUNDAY	

TOP PRIORITIES

VARIOUS TO DO

PEOPLE TO CONNECT WITH

PLACES TO VISIT

THINGS FOR NEXT WEEK

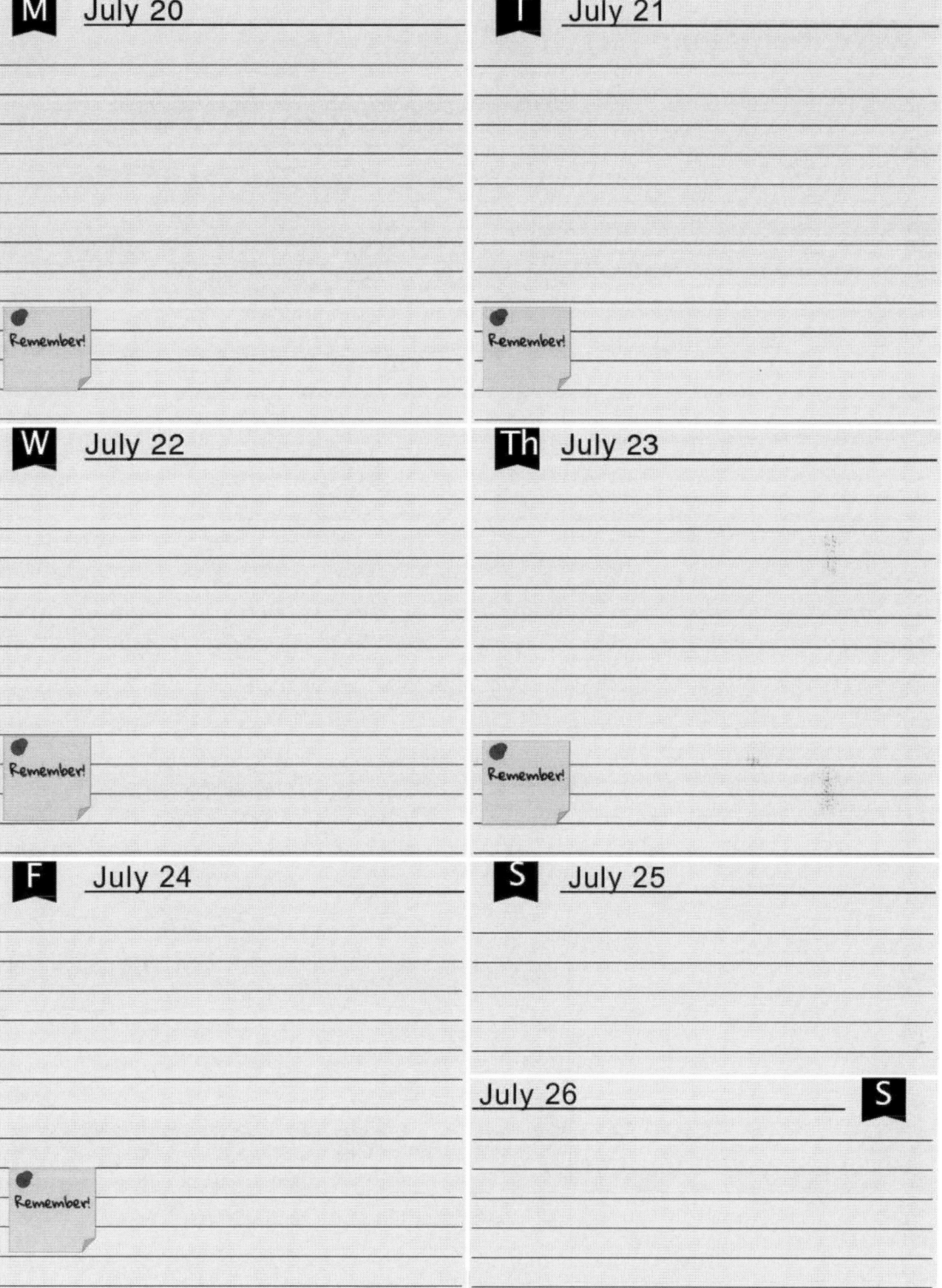

Week Beginning July 27, 2020

MONDAY	
TUESDAY	
WEDNESDAY	
THURSDAY	
FRIDAY	
SATURDAY	
SUNDAY	

TOP PRIORITIES

VARIOUS TO DO

PEOPLE TO CONNECT WITH

PLACES TO VISIT

THINGS FOR NEXT WEEK

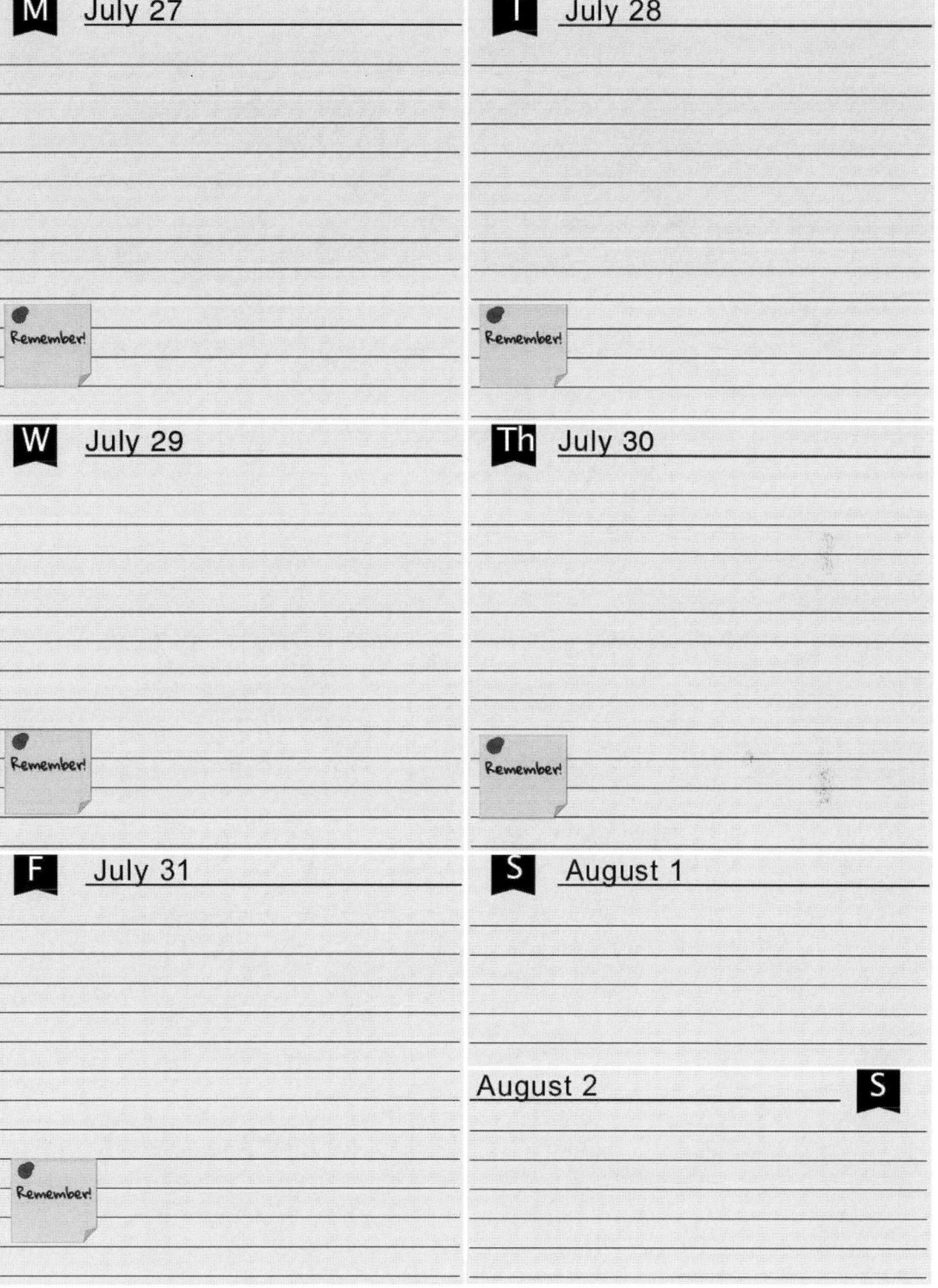

I AM THE BEST GUARD DOG. YOU CAN'T GET BY ME UNLESS YOU PET ME AND CALL ME A GOOD BOI...
THEN YOU CAN PASS BY QUITE EASILY.

Notes...

Banana Peanut Butter Frozen Popsicles

Ingredients:
- 4 cups (32-ounce container) plain yogurt
- 1 large banana
- 4 tablespoons peanut butter
- Coconut or olive oil cooking spray
- Small treats for the popsicle sticks.

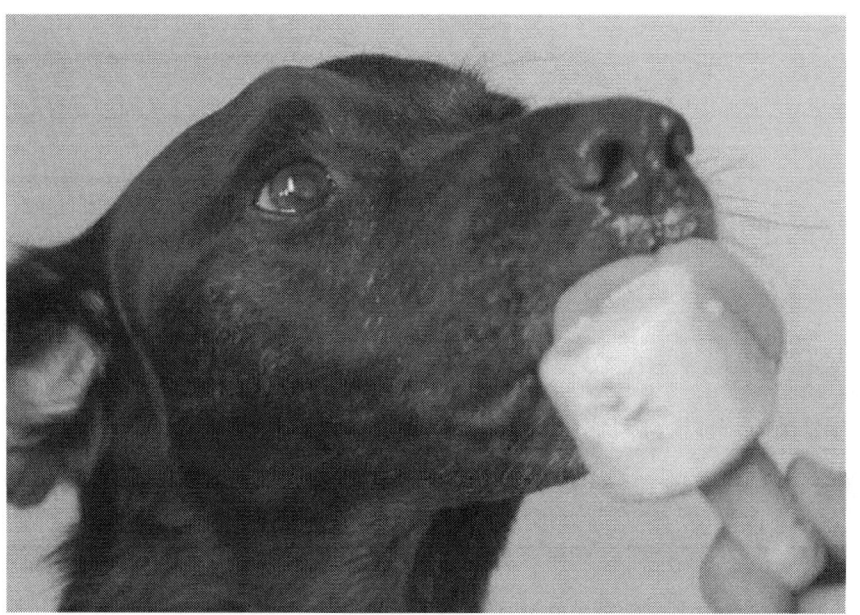

Instructions:

Blend yogurt, banana, and peanut butter in blender.

Place small cups in a rimmed baking pan and spray with cooking spray. (Instead of cups, you can use a silicone mold.)

Fill cups half way with yogurt mixture then place one treat in each cup to serve as an edible popsicle stick.

Transfer pan to freezer and freeze for 2 to 3 hours.

Remove a "pupsicle" from the freezer and hold onto the stick as your furry friend enjoys his treat. Once the frozen portion gets to be a manageable size, your dog can enjoy the treat on his own.

For dogs who are overeager and will want to chow these down right away, consider letting them soften a bit.

July Photo

Hardwood floors are not ideal for doin' the zoomies. No traction anywhere. This situation needs to be remedied, hooman.

EAR FLAPS STUCK IN THE COUCH!

AUGUST 2020

Sun	Mon	Tue	Wed	Thu	Fri	Sat
26	27	28	29	30	31	1
2	3	4	5	6	7	8
9	10	11	12	13	14	15
16	17	18	19	20	21	22
23	24	25	26	27	28	29
30	31	1	2	3	4	5

Notes:

Week Beginning August 3, 2020

MONDAY	
TUESDAY	
WEDNESDAY	
THURSDAY	
FRIDAY	
SATURDAY	
SUNDAY	

TOP PRIORITIES

VARIOUS TO DO

PEOPLE TO CONNECT WITH

PLACES TO VISIT

THINGS FOR NEXT WEEK

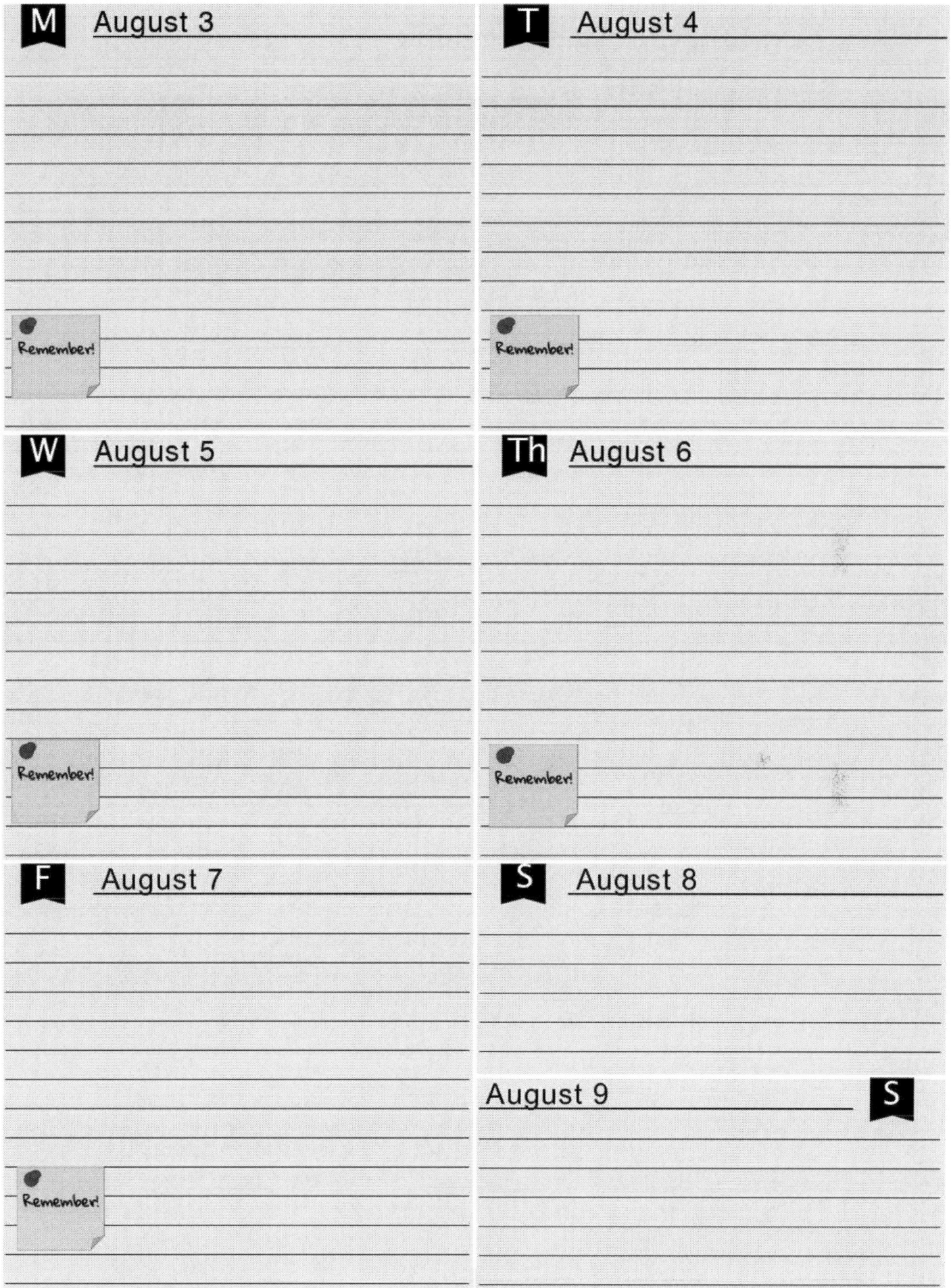

Week Beginning August 10, 2020

MONDAY

TUESDAY

WEDNESDAY

THURSDAY

FRIDAY

SATURDAY

SUNDAY

---------------- TOP PRIORITIES ----------------

VARIOUS TO DO

PEOPLE TO CONNECT WITH

PLACES TO VISIT

THINGS FOR NEXT WEEK

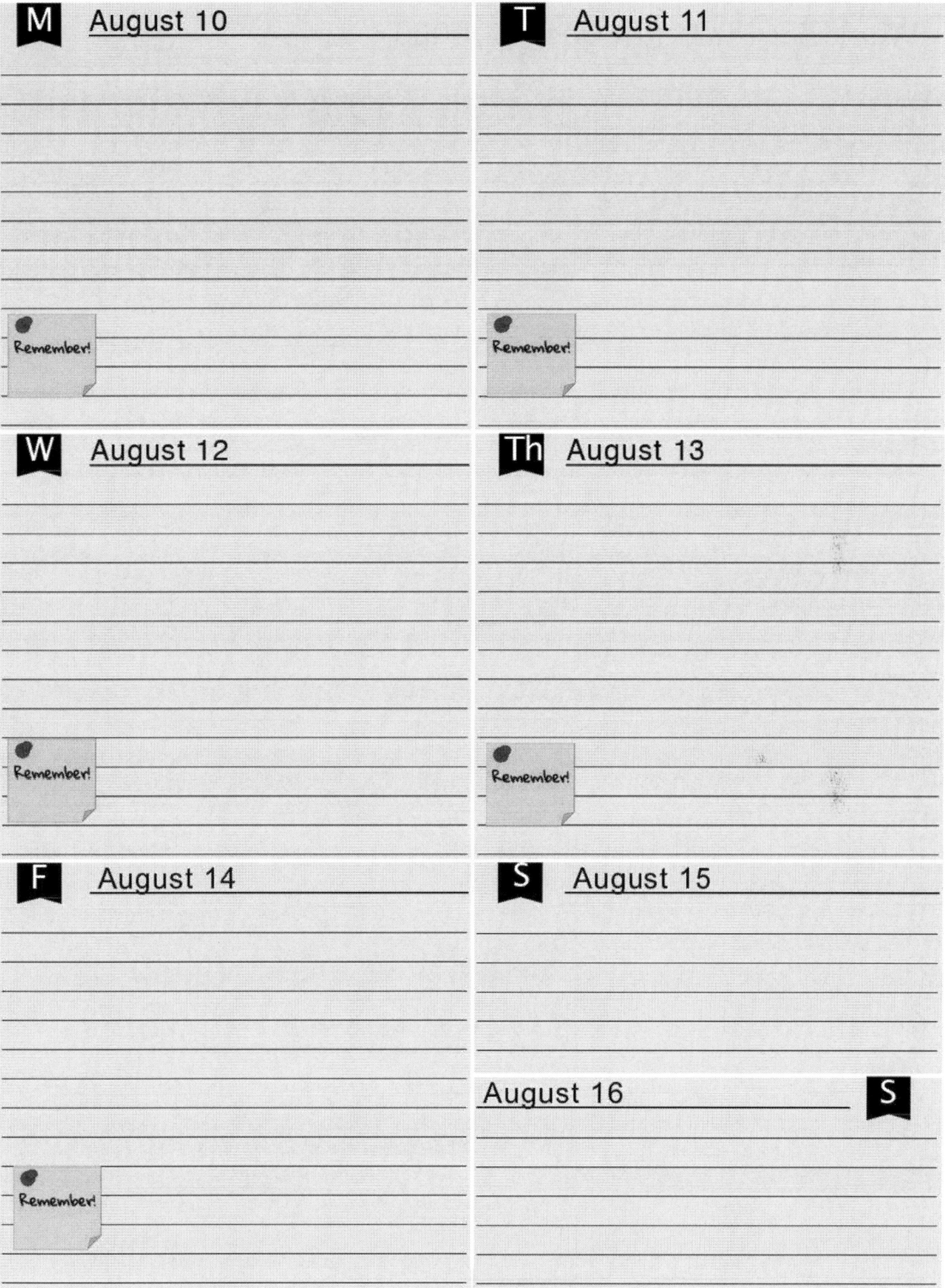

Week Beginning August 17, 2020

MONDAY	
TUESDAY	
WEDNESDAY	
THURSDAY	
FRIDAY	
SATURDAY	
SUNDAY	

TOP PRIORITIES

VARIOUS TO DO

PEOPLE TO CONNECT WITH

PLACES TO VISIT

THINGS FOR NEXT WEEK

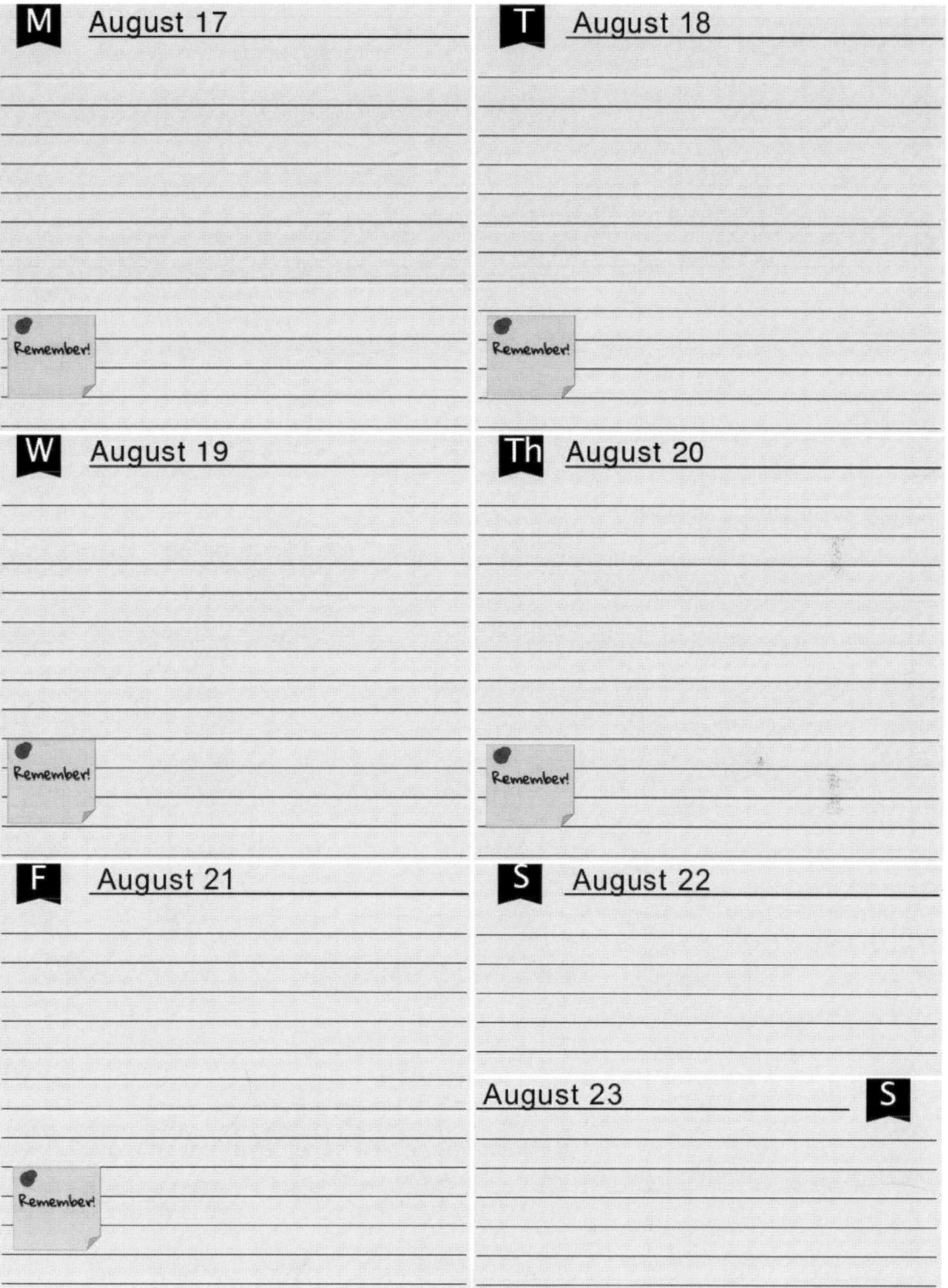

Week Beginning August 24, 2020

MONDAY	
TUESDAY	
WEDNESDAY	
THURSDAY	
FRIDAY	
SATURDAY	
SUNDAY	

TOP PRIORITIES

VARIOUS TO DO

PEOPLE TO CONNECT WITH

PLACES TO VISIT

THINGS FOR NEXT WEEK

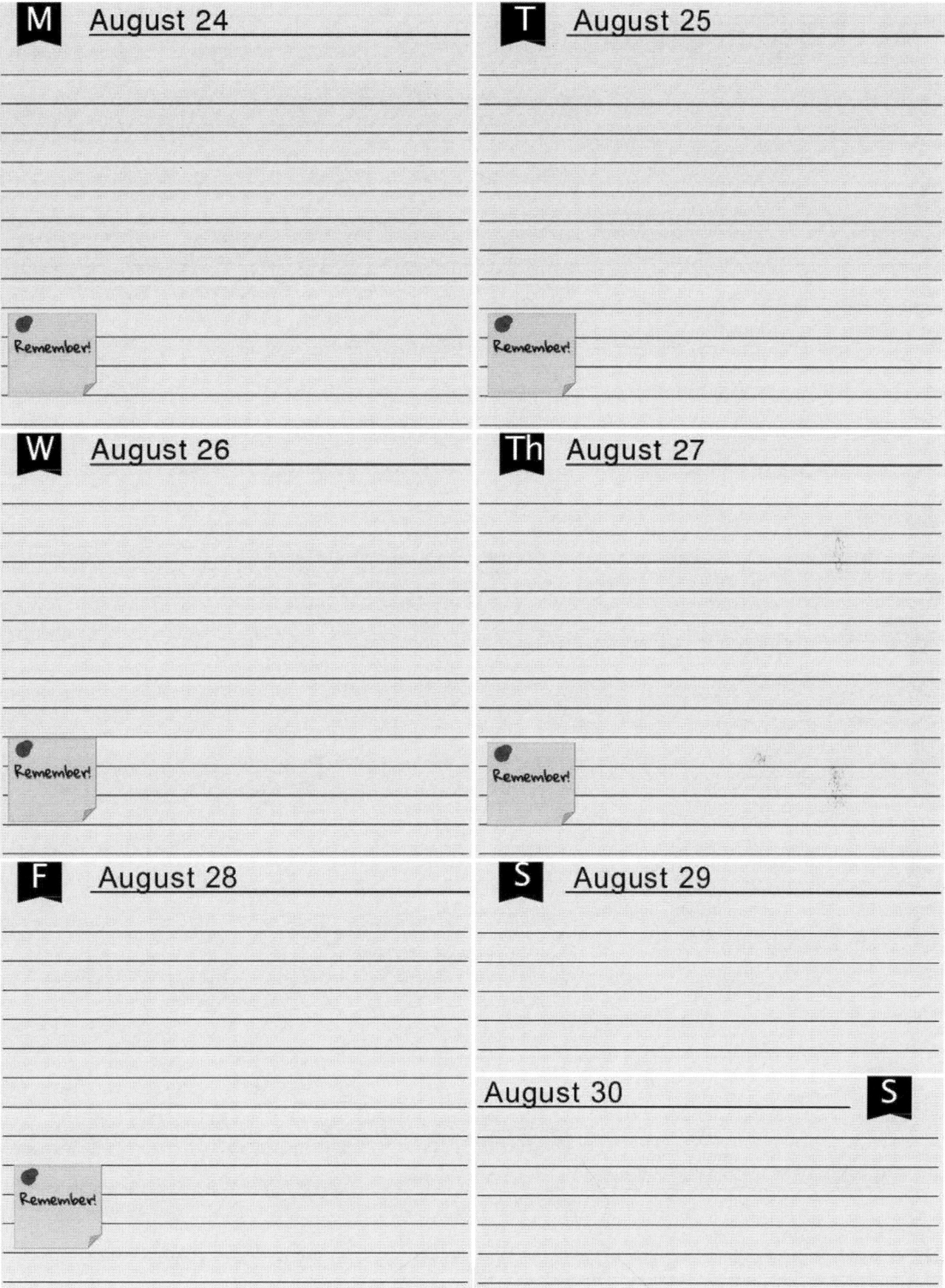

Week Beginning August 31, 2020

MONDAY	
TUESDAY	
WEDNESDAY	
THURSDAY	
FRIDAY	
SATURDAY	
SUNDAY	

TOP PRIORITIES

VARIOUS TO DO

PEOPLE TO CONNECT WITH

PLACES TO VISIT

THINGS FOR NEXT WEEK

M August 31

T September 1

Remember!

Remember!

W September 2

Th September 3

Remember!

Remember!

F September 4

S September 5

September 6 **S**

Remember!

My fren and me love:
...good tail wags
...cheese & chimkin
...invading your space
chasing Bruce - the lizard
peanut butter (oh yes!!!)
Speedy zoomies

Notes…

Spoiled Dog Birthday Cake

Ingredients:

Cake
- 1 cup flour
- 1/2 tsp baking soda
- 1/8 cup vegetable oil
- 1/4 cup peanut butter
- 1/2 cup applesauce
- 1/2 cup pumpkin puree
- 1 egg

Frosting
- 1/2 cup plain Greek yogurt
- 1/4 cup peanut butter

NATIONAL SPOIL YOUR DOG DAY
Monday, August 20, 2020

Instructions:

Cake

Preheat oven to 350 degrees F.

In a large bowl, combine flour and baking soda.

In a separate bowl mix together vegetable oil, peanut butter, applesauce and pumpkin puree. Once combined, mix in egg and mix until combined.

Combine wet and dry ingredients and stir until combined.

Pour mixture into an 8" round pan (a square pan can also be used) that has been greased with oil.

Bake for approximately 25-30 minutes or until a toothpick inserted into the center comes out clean and the cake springs back when pressed lightly.

Cake
Allow to cool on a wire rack prior to removing from pan.

After cooling, add frosting if desired.

Frosting
Mix Greek yogurt and peanut butter until well combined. Spread over cake. If not serving immediately, store in refrigerator.

August Photo

Bruce, the lizard, is staring at me through the screen door. "Bring it on, young doggo."

DOIN' ME A FRIGHTEN!

SEPTEMBER

I CALL MY DOG EGYPT BECAUSE HE LEAVES A PYRAMID IN EACH ROOM

SEPTEMBER 2020

Sun	Mon	Tue	Wed	Thu	Fri	Sat
30	31	1	2	3	4	5
6	7	8	9	10	11	12
13	14	15	16	17	18	19
20	21	22	23	24	25	26
27	28	29	30	1	2	3

Notes:

Week Beginning September 7, 2020

MONDAY	**TOP PRIORITIES**
TUESDAY	**VARIOUS TO DO**
WEDNESDAY	
THURSDAY	
FRIDAY	**PEOPLE TO CONNECT WITH**
SATURDAY	**PLACES TO VISIT**
SUNDAY	**THINGS FOR NEXT WEEK**

M September 7

Remember!

T September 8

Remember!

W September 9

Remember!

Th September 10

Remember!

F September 11

Remember!

S September 12

September 13 **S**

Week Beginning September 14, 2020

MONDAY	
TUESDAY	
WEDNESDAY	
THURSDAY	
FRIDAY	
SATURDAY	
SUNDAY	

TOP PRIORITIES

VARIOUS TO DO

PEOPLE TO CONNECT WITH

PLACES TO VISIT

THINGS FOR NEXT WEEK

M September 14

Remember!

T September 15

Remember!

W September 16

Remember!

Th September 17

Remember!

F September 18

Remember!

S September 19

September 20 **S**

Week Beginning September 21, 2020

	MONDAY
	TUESDAY
	WEDNESDAY
	THURSDAY
	FRIDAY
	SATURDAY
	SUNDAY

TOP PRIORITIES

VARIOUS TO DO

PEOPLE TO CONNECT WITH

PLACES TO VISIT

THINGS FOR NEXT WEEK

| **M** September 21 | **T** September 22 |

Remember!

| **W** September 23 | **Th** September 24 |

Remember!

| **F** September 25 | **S** September 26 |

September 27 **S**

Remember!

Week Beginning September 28, 2020

MONDAY

TUESDAY

WEDNESDAY

THURSDAY

FRIDAY

SATURDAY

SUNDAY

---------- TOP PRIORITIES ----------

VARIOUS TO DO

PEOPLE TO CONNECT WITH

PLACES TO VISIT

THINGS FOR NEXT WEEK

M September 28

T September 29

W September 30

Th October 1

F October 2

S October 3

October 4 **S**

These are my frens...we are all good bois.
...we love zoomies
...we bork
But only to protect you
..we love, we listen
...we love some more.
Is there any chimkin?

Notes…

Sweet Potato Fries Treats

Ingredients:
- 1 Sweet Potato
- 1 tbsp Coconut Oil (melted)
- Spices - Turmeric, Cinnamon

Instructions:

Preheat oven to 425 degrees F.

Wash and peel the sweet potato.

Cut the sweet potato into evenly sized long skinny (fry shaped) pieces.

Coat with oil and spices - Mix in a large bowl or Ziploc bag.

Place fries on baking sheet in one layer.

Bake for 15 minutes.

Flip over fries for even baking.

Bake for another 10-15 minutes.

Let cool before giving to your dog!

Dog Safe Spices
Basil, Cinnamon
Coriander, Dill
Ginger, Marjoram
Oregano, Parsley,
Rosemary, Sage
Tarragon, Thyme
Turmeric

September Photo

If I am ignored, I will notify the hooman via a series of discreet borfs. The offender will then be removed from the house.

IMMEDIATELY!

OCTOBER

> DOGS DO SPEAK BUT ONLY TO THOSE WHO KNOW HOW TO LISTEN

OCTOBER 2020

Sun	Mon	Tue	Wed	Thu	Fri	Sat
27	28	29	30	1	2	3
4	5	6	7	8	9	10
11	12	13	14	15	16	17
18	19	20	21	22	23	24
25	26	27	28	29	30	31

Notes:

Week Beginning October 5, 2020

MONDAY	
TUESDAY	
WEDNESDAY	
THURSDAY	
FRIDAY	
SATURDAY	
SUNDAY	

TOP PRIORITIES

VARIOUS TO DO

PEOPLE TO CONNECT WITH

PLACES TO VISIT

THINGS FOR NEXT WEEK

M October 5

T October 6

Remember!

Remember!

W October 7

Th October 8

Remember!

Remember!

F October 9

S October 10

October 11 **S**

Remember!

Week Beginning October 12, 2020

MONDAY

TUESDAY

WEDNESDAY

THURSDAY

FRIDAY

SATURDAY

SUNDAY

---------- TOP PRIORITIES ----------

VARIOUS TO DO

PEOPLE TO CONNECT WITH

PLACES TO VISIT

THINGS FOR NEXT WEEK

M October 12

Remember!

T October 13

Remember!

W October 14

Remember!

Th October 15

Remember!

F October 16

Remember!

S October 17

October 18 **S**

Week Beginning October 19, 2020

MONDAY	
TUESDAY	
WEDNESDAY	
THURSDAY	
FRIDAY	
SATURDAY	
SUNDAY	

TOP PRIORITIES

VARIOUS TO DO

PEOPLE TO CONNECT WITH

PLACES TO VISIT

THINGS FOR NEXT WEEK

M October 19

T October 20

Remember!

Remember!

W October 21

Th October 22

Remember!

Remember!

F October 23

S October 24

October 25 **S**

Remember!

Week Beginning October 26, 2020

	MONDAY
	TUESDAY
	WEDNESDAY
	THURSDAY
	FRIDAY
	SATURDAY
	SUNDAY

TOP PRIORITIES

VARIOUS TO DO

PEOPLE TO CONNECT WITH

PLACES TO VISIT

THINGS FOR NEXT WEEK

M October 26

Remember!

T October 27

Remember!

W October 28

Remember!

Th October 29

Remember!

F October 30

Remember!

S October 31

November 1 **S**

MY FREN AND ME ARE GETTING ALONG REAL WELL. WE ALTERNATE BORKS, WOOFS AND GRRBORKS

FOR ULTIMATE PROTECT.

Notes…

Pumpkin Apple Dog Treats

Ingredients:
- 4 - 4.5 cups oatmeal, plus additional
- 1 medium apple
- 1 egg
- 1 CUP canned pumpkin

Instructions:

Preheat oven to 400 degrees F.

Grind the oatmeal down in a food processor or blender. Transfer to mixing bowl.

Core apple, being sure to remove all of the seeds. Grate apple, and add to bowl with oatmeal.

Add egg and canned pumpkin to bowl and mix well to combine. The mixture will be thick and slightly sticky.

On a surface dusted with oatmeal (ground or not, your choice) roll the dough out to approximately 1/2" thick. Use a doggy bone cookie cutter to cut dough into shapes, and transfer to a lined baking sheet.

Bake for approximately 12-15 minutes, or until golden and crispy. Allow to cool to room temperature, then store in an airtight container for up to a week.

October Photo

Some say a dog's life is easy...no worries, no taxes. I say, walk a mile in my shoes. That reminds me, I took your shoe.

SORRY, HOOMAN!

NOVEMBER

THE ROAD TO MY HEART IS PAVED WITH PAW PRINTS

NOVEMBER 2020

Sun	Mon	Tue	Wed	Thu	Fri	Sat
1	2	3	4	5	6	7
8	9	10	11	12	13	14
15	16	17	18	19	20	21
22	23	24	25	26	27	28
29	30	1	2	3	4	5

Notes:

Week Beginning November 2, 2020

MONDAY	
TUESDAY	
WEDNESDAY	
THURSDAY	
FRIDAY	
SATURDAY	
SUNDAY	

TOP PRIORITIES

VARIOUS TO DO

PEOPLE TO CONNECT WITH

PLACES TO VISIT

THINGS FOR NEXT WEEK

M November 2

Remember!

T November 3

Remember!

W November 4

Remember!

Th November 5

Remember!

F November 6

Remember!

S November 7

November 8 S

Week Beginning November 9, 2020

MONDAY	
TUESDAY	
WEDNESDAY	
THURSDAY	
FRIDAY	
SATURDAY	
SUNDAY	

TOP PRIORITIES

VARIOUS TO DO

PEOPLE TO CONNECT WITH

PLACES TO VISIT

THINGS FOR NEXT WEEK

M November 9

Remember!

T November 10

Remember!

W November 11

Remember!

Th November 12

Remember!

F November 13

Remember!

S November 14

November 15 **S**

Week Beginning November 16, 2020

MONDAY	
TUESDAY	
WEDNESDAY	
THURSDAY	
FRIDAY	
SATURDAY	
SUNDAY	

TOP PRIORITIES

VARIOUS TO DO

PEOPLE TO CONNECT WITH

PLACES TO VISIT

THINGS FOR NEXT WEEK

M November 16

Remember!

T November 17

Remember!

W November 18

Remember!

Th November 19

Remember!

F November 20

Remember!

S November 21

November 22 **S**

Week Beginning November 23, 2020

	MONDAY	TUESDAY	WEDNESDAY	THURSDAY	FRIDAY	SATURDAY	SUNDAY

TOP PRIORITIES

VARIOUS TO DO

PEOPLE TO CONNECT WITH

PLACES TO VISIT

THINGS FOR NEXT WEEK

M November 23

T November 24

W November 25

Th November 26

F November 27

S November 28

November 29 **S**

Remember!

Week Beginning November 30, 2020

MONDAY	
TUESDAY	
WEDNESDAY	
THURSDAY	
FRIDAY	
SATURDAY	
SUNDAY	

TOP PRIORITIES

VARIOUS TO DO

PEOPLE TO CONNECT WITH

PLACES TO VISIT

THINGS FOR NEXT WEEK

M November 30

Remember!

T December 1

Remember!

W December 2

Remember!

Th December 3

Remember!

F December 4

Remember!

S December 5

December 6 **S**

SIMON, THE PESKY CAT WAS STARING AT ME THROUGH THE WINDOW...ALL DAY.

I BORKED AND GRRBORKED AND WOOFED...BUT HE APPEARS TO BE HECKIN' DEAF.

Notes…

Grain-Free Dog Treats

Ingredients:
- 2 cups coconut flour
- ½ teaspoon baking soda
- ½ teaspoon cinnamon
- 1 can 15 oz. pure pumpkin
- ½ cup peanut butter
- ½ cup coconut oil melted
- 4 eggs

Peanut Butter Drizzle:
- 1/3 cup peanut butter
- 1-2 tablespoons melted coconut oil

Instructions:

Preheat oven to 350 degrees F.

Add eggs to large bowl and beat. Add the remaining ingredients and stir together until a soft dough forms.

Place on parchment paper and carefully roll dough out with a rolling pin (you may need to put another piece of parchment paper on top so it doesn't stick to rolling pin).

Cut dough into shapes with cookie cutters and gently transfer to baking sheet lined with parchment paper.

Bake for 12 to 18 minutes, or until treats are hard. Remove from oven and cool for 5 minutes on baking sheet. Transfer to cooling rack.

For peanut butter drizzle, combine melted coconut oil and peanut butter and drizzle over treats.

Store in airtight container at room temperature or in the refrigerator up to one week. Store in the freezer for a month.

November Photo

My most fancy tricks...
Snoozing, sit (a classic), the fetch, trot/advanced walk, roll, zoom (speedy), begging for chimkin.

SORTED BY DIFFICULTY!

DECEMBER

My little dog — a heartbeat at my feet

DECEMBER 2020

Sun	Mon	Tue	Wed	Thu	Fri	Sat
29	30	1	2	3	4	5
6	7	8	9	10	11	12
13	14	15	16	17	18	19
20	21	22	23	24	25	26
27	28	29	30	31	1	2

Notes:

Week Beginning December 7, 2020

MONDAY

TUESDAY

WEDNESDAY

THURSDAY

FRIDAY

SATURDAY

SUNDAY

TOP PRIORITIES

VARIOUS TO DO

PEOPLE TO CONNECT WITH

PLACES TO VISIT

THINGS FOR NEXT WEEK

M December 7

Remember!

T December 8

Remember!

W December 9

Remember!

Th December 10

Remember!

F December 11

Remember!

S December 12

December 13 **S**

Week Beginning December 14, 2020

MONDAY	
TUESDAY	
WEDNESDAY	
THURSDAY	
FRIDAY	
SATURDAY	
SUNDAY	

TOP PRIORITIES

VARIOUS TO DO

PEOPLE TO CONNECT WITH

PLACES TO VISIT

THINGS FOR NEXT WEEK

M December 14

Remember!

T December 15

Remember!

W December 16

Remember!

Th December 17

Remember!

F December 18

Remember!

S December 19

December 20 **S**

Week Beginning December 21, 2020

MONDAY	
TUESDAY	
WEDNESDAY	
THURSDAY	
FRIDAY	
SATURDAY	
SUNDAY	

TOP PRIORITIES

VARIOUS TO DO

PEOPLE TO CONNECT WITH

PLACES TO VISIT

THINGS FOR NEXT WEEK

M December 21

T December 22

Remember!

Remember!

W December 23

Th December 24

Remember!

Remember!

F December 25

S December 26

December 27 **S**

Remember!

Week Beginning December 28, 2020

MONDAY	
TUESDAY	
WEDNESDAY	
THURSDAY	
FRIDAY	
SATURDAY	
SUNDAY	

TOP PRIORITIES

VARIOUS TO DO

PEOPLE TO CONNECT WITH

PLACES TO VISIT

THINGS FOR NEXT WEEK

M December 28

Remember!

T December 29

Remember!

W December 30

Remember!

Th December 31

Remember!

F January 1 (2021)

Remember!

S January 2

January 3 **S**

WOOF NEW FRENS!

I just had the best walk ever! I saw 35 or 4 other dogs.... woofers, thick bois, a loaf, even a floofer pupper. Life is good!

Notes…

Peppermint Holi-Dog Treats

Ingredients:
- 3 cups whole wheat flour
- 1 cup water
- 1 tsp molasses
- 2 Tbs peanut butter
- 2 Tbs olive oil
- 1 tsp peppermint extract

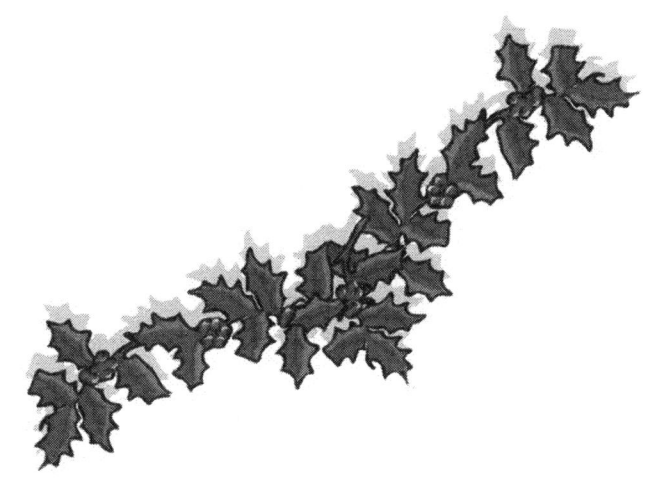

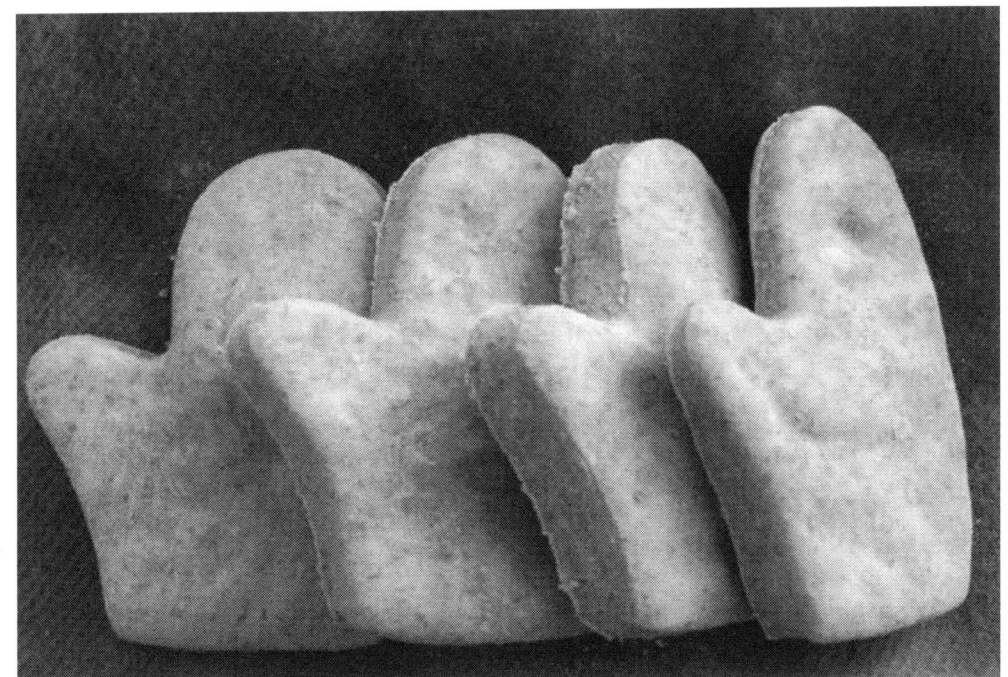

Instructions:

Preheat oven to 350 degrees.

In a large bowl, mix flour, molasses, peanut butter, water, olive oil and peppermint extract until smooth.

Kneed flour on a floured surface and roll out to ¼ inch thickness. Cut with festive cookie cutters and place on non-stick cookie sheets.

Bake for 30 minutes. Cool on wire rack. Store treats in a sealed container and refrigerate or freeze.

December Photo

The hooman said we could go on a car ride tomorrow when he gets home. I'm so happy, I can't even snooze.

TAIL IS WAGGING SO FAST!

Made in the USA
Columbia, SC
03 December 2020